This story is dedicated
to my grandchildren,
Orion and Izel Romberg

# In Memory of Cricket

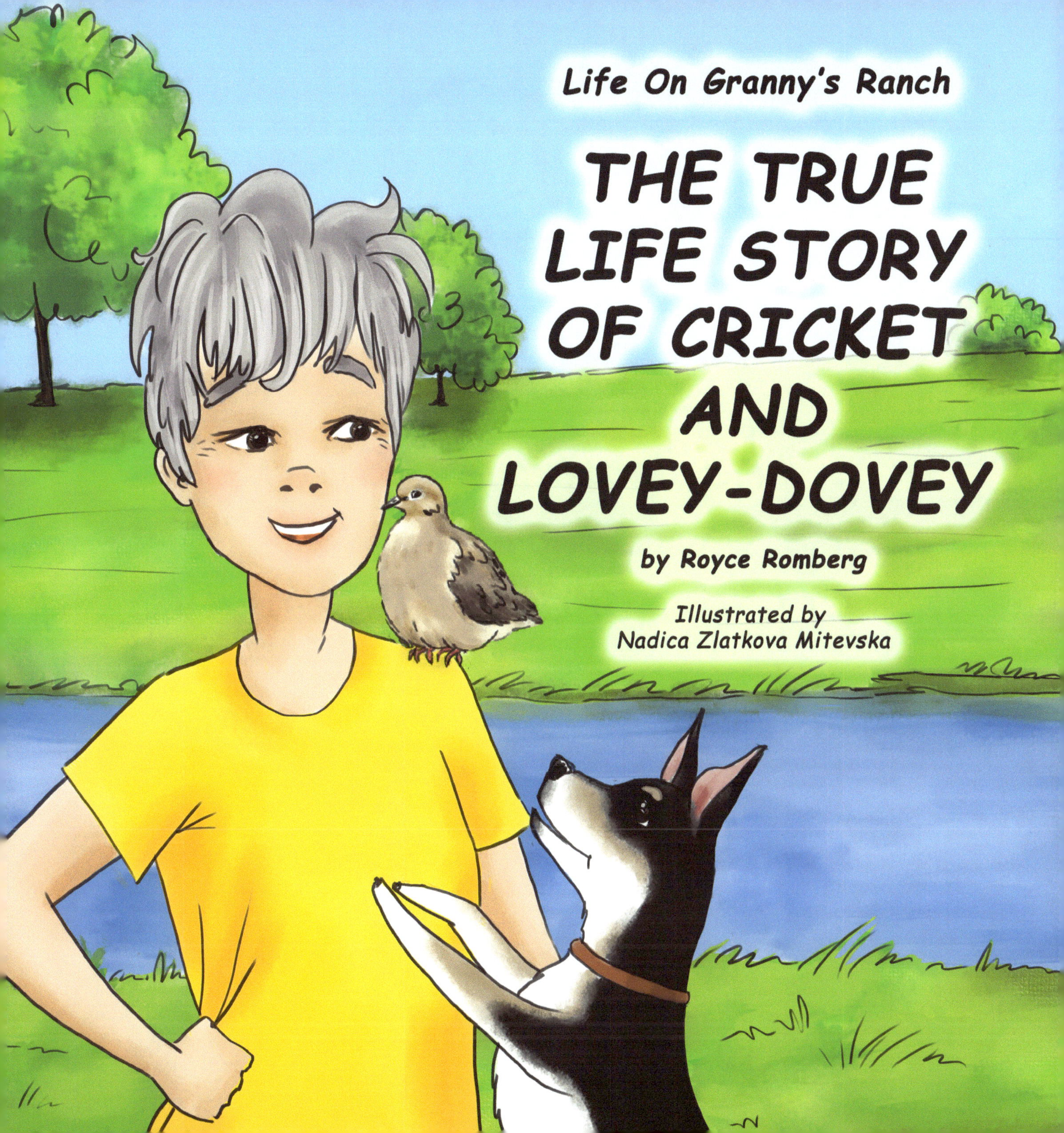

Life On Granny's Ranch
THE TRUE LIFE STORY OF CRICKET AND LOVEY-DOVEY
by Royce Romberg
Illustrated by Nadica Zlatkova Mitevska

# The True Life Story
## of
## Cricket and Lovey-Dovey

Early one summer morning, just as the sun peaked over the tank,
Cricket, the dog, and Granny walked to the barn
to feed all the animals - just like they always did.

Granny started feeding and Cricket headed out to patrol the ranch
for animal intruders, like raccoons, skunks, or snakes.

When Granny had finished feeding the pig, horses, cows and cats, she called for Cricket to come to breakfast, but she didn't come.

Granny looked and looked and looked
and finally saw her way at the back of the barn, playing.
Granny shrugged - figuring she was playing with a mouse,
or snake, or a kitten - and went in for coffee.

Two hours later Cricket was still in the back of the barn
so Granny went to check on her. To her surprise, Cricket was not alone.
She was laying on her stomach with a baby bird between her front legs.

When Granny called, Cricket came bounding over with excitement,
leaving the baby bird alone. That was when one of the barn cats,
Zebra, started to move in on the birdie.
He slunk over, tail twitching, about to pounce on the baby bird
(That's what cats do). Cricket ran back over and stood over the baby bird,
protecting it and scaring Zebra away.

Granny fussed at Zebra and shooed him away then picked up the baby bird. She looked at Cricket and said, "What should we do with the baby?" Cricket trotted down the barn aisle and stopped in front of the baby duck pen. Granny thought that was a great idea, and she and Cricket made  a nice nest with hay in a box with some seeds and water.

After supper Granny got on the computer and googled
the picture she had taken and discovered it was a baby dove.
Doves are very friendly, she told Cricket.
Let's name her Lovey-Dovey.Cricket barked her approval.
Granny smiled at Cricket and told her
that they would look for Lovey's family the next day.

The next morning, Granny and Cricket
took Lovey to the back of the barn
where Cricket had found her.
Granny looked up and saw
a nest way at the top of the barn.
2 doves sat beside it—Mom and Dad.
They cooed to Lovey who cooed back
(That's how doves talk to each other).
Granny tried to get Lovey to fly
by lightly tossing her in the air
but she was still too young.
She couldn't fly but a few feet.

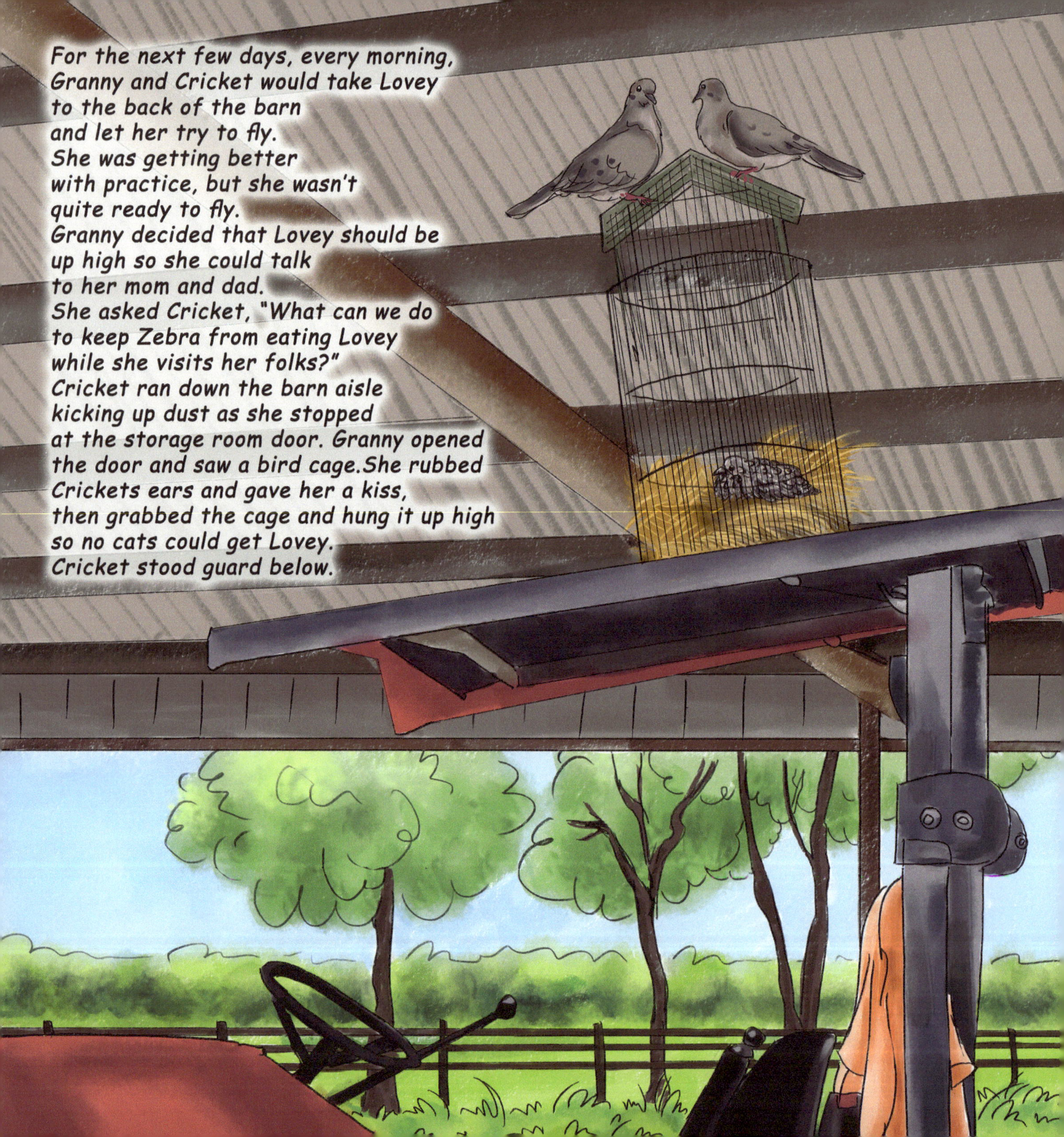

For the next few days, every morning,
Granny and Cricket would take Lovey
to the back of the barn
and let her try to fly.
She was getting better
with practice, but she wasn't
quite ready to fly.
Granny decided that Lovey should be
up high so she could talk
to her mom and dad.
She asked Cricket, "What can we do
to keep Zebra from eating Lovey
while she visits her folks?"
Cricket ran down the barn aisle
kicking up dust as she stopped
at the storage room door. Granny opened
the door and saw a bird cage.She rubbed
Crickets ears and gave her a kiss,
then grabbed the cage and hung it up high
so no cats could get Lovey.
Cricket stood guard below.

One morning Granny and Cricket went to the duck pen to feed
and Lovey was gone. They were very sad and worried that something
had happened to her. But, after looking all around, they gave up.
Granny told Cricket that Lovey must have learned to fly
and flew off to be with her family.

That afternoon, Granny heard Cricket barking in the back of the barn.
She walked back to see what all the commotion was about.
Cricket was looking up and barking. There was Lovey-Dovey,
back in her nest at the top of the barn.

Lovey still lives in the barn and visits Granny and Cricket every day.

Royce Romberg is a 73 year old rancher in Central Texas. She graduated from The University of Texas with a degree in Journalism. On her ranch Royce has dogs, cats, horses, cows, llamas, ducks, a pot belly pig, a donkey and many visitors like raccoons, possums, snakes, bobcats and lots of birds.

Since she was a little girl, Royce has loved animals. As a child, she had a dog named Doggus and was always bringing home strays.

When the Rombergs started their family, along with 3 kids, they had 50 animals - dogs, cats, horses, goats, ferrets, chinchillas, hedgehogs, hamsters and goldfish. Royce's motto has always been, "The more the merrier!"